Learn Symfony

Practical Guide

A. De Quattro

Copyright © 2024

Guide to Symfony

1. Introduction to Symfony

Symfony is an open-source PHP framework used for developing complex and scalable web applications. Created in 2005 by Fabien Potencier, Symfony has become one of the most popular and widely used PHP frameworks in the web development industry.

Symfony is designed to help developers create robust and maintainable web applications, following the principles of the Model-View-Controller (MVC) design pattern and promoting best software development practices. With its modular and flexible architecture, Symfony allows developers to work efficiently and productively, minimizing code duplication and facilitating application maintenance over time.

One of Symfony's distinctive features is the concept of bundles, which allow developers to organize code into separate and reusable modules, facilitating the management of application features and collaboration among development team members. Additionally, Symfony offers a wide ecosystem of pre-defined bundles and third-party packages, enabling developers to extend the framework's functionalities and easily integrate external technologies.

Symfony is built on several core components, including routing, controller, form, security, templating, and database, providing powerful and flexible tools for managing various application development needs. With its detailed documentation and active developer community, Symfony is easy to learn and use, even for beginners in web development.

In this article, we will delve into the key features and functionalities of Symfony, examining its capabilities and advantages in the context of modern and complex web application development. We will explore the framework's core components in detail, illustrating how to use them to create high-performance, scalable, and maintainable web applications. Finally, we will also examine some common use cases of Symfony and its integration possibilities with other technologies and platforms.

Core Components of Symfony

Symfony consists of several core components that provide essential base functionalities for web application development. Each component is designed to perform a specific task and can be used individually or combined with other components to create complex and customized web applications. The main components of Symfony are listed below:

1. Routing: Symfony's routing component manages the routing of HTTP requests within the application, associating a URL with a specific controller. With Symfony's routing system, developers can define custom rules

for handling routes and associated parameters, allowing the creation of meaningful and semantic URLs for various application pages.

2. Controller: Symfony's controller component manages the business logic of the application, processing HTTP requests received from the browser and generating appropriate responses. Symfony controllers are PHP classes that contain methods to handle various application actions, such as displaying pages, handling forms, and manipulating database data.

3. Form: Symfony's form component provides an intuitive and flexible system for creating and managing HTML forms within the application. With Symfony's form system, developers can easily define input fields, data validations, error messages, and data handling actions, simplifying the creation of complex and interactive forms for the user.

4. Security: Symfony's security component provides advanced functionality for managing authentication, authorization, and application resource protection. With Symfony's security system, developers can define custom access rules, manage user sessions, and implement encryption mechanisms to protect the application's sensitive data.

5. Templating: Symfony's templating component handles the display of application data through the use of HTML and CSS templates. With Symfony's templating system, developers can easily create customized page layouts, integrate PHP scripts, and include dynamic components within the application pages.

6. Database: Symfony's database component provides a unified interface for managing database access operations within the application. With Symfony's database system, developers can easily create SQL queries, manage transactions, and interact with various

types of databases, such as MySQL, PostgreSQL, and SQLite.

These are just some of Symfony's core components, providing essential functionalities for web application development. In addition to these components, Symfony offers a wide range of third-party bundles and packages, allowing developers to further extend the framework's functionalities and integrate external technologies, such as REST APIs, cloud services, and caching systems.

Advantages of Symfony

Symfony offers numerous advantages and benefits for developers who choose to use it for creating web applications. Some of the key advantages of Symfony include:

1. High productivity: Symfony offers

powerful and flexible tools for creating complex and scalable web applications, allowing developers to work efficiently and productively. With its modular architecture and rich documentation, Symfony simplifies the management of various stages of application development and reduces the time required to complete projects.

2. Maintainability: Symfony promotes best software development practices, such as separation of concerns and code duplication reduction, which facilitate the creation of easily maintainable web applications over time. With its well-structured architecture and automated testing features, Symfony makes it easier to debug and fix errors in the application, ensuring greater stability and reliability of the software.

3. Scalability: Symfony is designed to handle high-traffic web applications and large volumes of data, offering high-performance and scalable solutions in case of increased

demand. With its modular architecture and integrated caching system, Symfony allows developers to optimize application performance and effectively manage workload growth over time.

4. Security: Symfony provides an advanced security system to protect the application from vulnerabilities and external threats, such as hacker attacks, code injections, and data theft. With its advanced authentication and authorization system, Symfony enables developers to implement robust security measures and ensure the protection of the application's data.

5. Active community: Symfony boasts a vast and active community of developers and industry professionals who share knowledge, experiences, and resources to help developers grow and improve their skills. With its dynamic and collaborative community, Symfony offers technical support, regular updates, and educational resources to help

developers make the most of the framework and stay up-to-date on the latest industry trends.

Use Cases of Symfony

Symfony is used in a wide range of contexts and industries for creating various types of web applications, such as corporate websites, e-commerce platforms, content management portals, SaaS applications, and more. Some of the main use cases of Symfony include:

1. Corporate websites: Symfony is widely used for developing corporate websites and content portals, thanks to its flexibility, scalability, and advanced security features. Developers can use Symfony to create and manage customized websites tailored to the specific needs of businesses, integrating functionalities such as content management, analytics tracking, user management, and more.

2. E-commerce platforms: Symfony is often used for developing e-commerce platforms and online stores, thanks to its ability to handle large quantities of products, transactions, and users simultaneously. Developers can use Symfony to create customized online stores with advanced features, such as shopping carts, online payments, order management, and integrations with external payment systems.

3. SaaS applications: Symfony is ideal for developing Software as a Service (SaaS) applications, offering cloud-based services through monthly or annual subscriptions. Developers can use Symfony to create customizable and scalable SaaS applications that allow users to access online tools and resources from any device, anywhere in the world.

4. Public service web applications: Symfony

is commonly used for developing public service web applications, such as government websites, information platforms, and citizen support portals. Developers can use Symfony to create secure and reliable web applications that provide essential services and useful information to citizens and public institutions.

Integrations with other technologies

Symfony is designed to easily integrate with other technologies and platforms, allowing developers to create complex and scalable web applications that leverage the full potential of modern technologies. Some of the main integrations of Symfony include:

1. REST APIs: Symfony provides native support for creating RESTful APIs, allowing web applications to interact with external services and share data and resources through HTTP requests. Developers can use Symfony to create customized and scalable RESTful

APIs that meet the specific needs of the application and its users.

2. Cloud services: Symfony can be integrated with cloud services like AWS, Google Cloud Platform, and Microsoft Azure to obtain additional resources and manage application scalability. Developers can use Symfony to integrate external cloud services and leverage their advanced features, such as data storage, image processing, and data analysis.

3. Caching systems: Symfony offers an integrated caching system that allows developers to temporarily store application data to improve performance and reduce server load. Developers can use Symfony to integrate external caching systems, such as Redis and Memcached, to further optimize application performance and ensure fast responses to user requests.

4. Data analysis tools: Symfony can be

integrated with data analysis tools such as Apache Spark, Elasticsearch, and Splunk to gain deep insights into application activities and user behaviors. Developers can use Symfony to integrate external data analysis tools and improve the predictive and decision-making capabilities of the application.

Symfony is a powerful and flexible PHP framework that offers numerous advantages for developers who choose it for creating modern and scalable web applications. With its modular architecture and advanced features, Symfony allows developers to create high-performance and reliable web applications that meet the specific needs of their users and businesses.

Whether it's corporate websites, e-commerce platforms, SaaS applications, or online public services, Symfony offers essential tools and resources for the success of web projects. With its vast community of developers and industry professionals, Symfony provides technical support, regular updates, and educational resources to help developers grow and improve their skills and knowledge.

Symfony continues to be one of the most popular and widely used PHP frameworks in the web development industry, offering advanced features, high performance, and ease of use for successful web application development. If you are a developer looking to create complex and scalable web projects, Symfony could be the right choice for you.

2. Symfony Installation

Symfony is an open-source PHP framework and one of the most popular in the world. Thanks to its flexibility, scalability, and ease of use, Symfony is used by developers worldwide to create web applications of all kinds and sizes. In this article, we will explore how to install Symfony and start using it to create web projects.

Before proceeding with the installation of Symfony, it is important to ensure that the minimum system requirements are met. Symfony requires PHP 7.2.5 or higher, Composer, a dependency manager for PHP, and some PHP extensions such as PDO, PECL, and others that can be installed through Composer or manually via the terminal.

Once the minimum requirements are met, you can proceed with the installation of Symfony. There are several ways to install Symfony, including using the Symfony Installer, Composer, or the Symfony flex command. In this article, we will focus on installation via Composer, the most common and recommended method by Symfony developers.

To install Symfony via Composer, you need to open the terminal and type the following command:

```
composer create-project symfony/skeleton project-name
```

Where "project-name" can be replaced with the desired name for our project. This command will create a new directory with the project name and install Symfony along with the necessary dependencies inside it. Once the installation is complete, you can access the project directory and start the Symfony development server using the following command:

```
cd project-name
symfony server:start
```

This command will start a local server and allow you to view the Symfony project at localhost:8000 in the browser. Alternatively, you can start Symfony using a web server like Apache or Nginx configured with PHP.

Once the server is running, you can start working on the Symfony project. Symfony follows the principle of "convention over configuration," which means that many aspects of the framework are pre-configured following best web development practices.

The structure of a Symfony project follows an MVC (Model-View-Controller) pattern, with dedicated directories for controllers, templates, and models.

Symfony also offers a wide range of components and bundles that can be used to add functionality to the project. These components are often installed via Composer and can be configured and customized according to the project's needs.

Furthermore, Symfony offers a variety of command-line tools that simplify the development process. For example, the `bin/console make:controller` command allows you to easily create a new controller, while `bin/console make:entity` allows you to create a new entity for the database.

Symfony also provides a powerful routing system that allows you to easily define application routes and associate them with corresponding controllers. This way, you can create meaningful URLs and efficiently handle user requests.

Finally, Symfony also offers a robust security system that allows you to protect the application from external threats. By using components like the Guard Authentication System and the Security Bundle, you can easily manage user authentication and authorization in the application.

In conclusion, installing Symfony is a fairly simple process that requires a few steps and can be completed in a few minutes. Once installed, Symfony offers a wide range of features and tools that simplify the development of complex and advanced web applications. If you are a PHP programmer and are looking for a powerful and flexible framework for your web projects, Symfony could be the right choice for you. We hope that this article has provided you with the necessary information to start using Symfony and delve into its features.

3. Symfony's MVC Architecture

Symfony is an open-source PHP framework that allows the development of efficient and scalable web applications following the MVC (Model-View-Controller) architectural pattern. This pattern divides the application into three distinct parts: the Model, the View, and the Controller, each with specific roles and well-defined responsibilities. Using the MVC architecture with Symfony allows organizing the code clearly and modularly, facilitating maintenance and management of the application over time.

The Model represents the business logic of the application and manages data access. In Symfony, the Model is often represented by Doctrine entities, which represent database tables and contain the necessary data for the application. Doctrine entities can be defined through PHP annotations or configuration files in XML or YAML format. For example, a User entity could contain information such as the user's name, email, and password.

The Controller handles user requests and coordinates the actions of the Model and the View. In Symfony, Controllers are PHP classes that handle routing logic and process HTTP requests. An example of a Controller could be the UserController, which handles requests related to users, such as registering a new user or retrieving information about an existing user. Within a Controller, you can access the Model to retrieve and manipulate data and the View to return a response to the user.

The View is responsible for displaying data to the user in a comprehensive and pleasant format. In Symfony, Views are represented by Twig template files, a flexible and powerful template engine that allows easy integration of PHP code within HTML markup. Twig template files can contain variables and code blocks to handle data presentation based on information provided by the Controller. For example, a Twig template file to display user information could contain HTML code to format data retrieved from the Model.

Symfony's MVC architecture promotes task separation and code modularity, allowing the development of scalable and maintainable web applications. A practical example of implementing the MVC architecture in Symfony is creating a simple application for managing a list of users.

Let's start by defining the User entity, which will represent a user within the application. We can define the User entity using PHP annotations within a PHP class that extends Doctrine's BaseEntity class:

[PHP code for defining the User entity is provided]

Once the User entity is defined, we can

proceed with creating the UserController, which will handle user-related operations within the application. The UserController will manage operations such as viewing, creating, modifying, and deleting users, interacting with the User Model to access the necessary data.

[PHP code for defining the UserController and its methods is provided]

Lastly, we define Twig template files to display user data within the application. Using Twig, we can easily integrate PHP code within HTML markup to dynamically display data retrieved by the Controller. For example, we define a list.html.twig template file to display the list of users and a detail.html.twig template file to display details of a single user.

[Twig template code for list.html.twig and detail.html.twig is provided]

With this example, we have demonstrated how to use MVC architecture with Symfony to create a web application for managing a list of users, separating business logic (Model), data presentation (View), and user request handling (Controller) in a modular and clear manner. Symfony offers numerous tools and components to simplify the development of complex web applications, allowing the creation of efficient and scalable applications while maintaining organized and maintainable code.

4. Symfony Services and Containers

In Symfony, services are objects that perform specific tasks within an application. They can be used to execute business logic operations, communicate with external databases, send emails, make API calls, and much more. Services are widely used in Symfony to keep code well-structured, modularized, and easily testable.

A related concept to services in Symfony is that of service containers. The service container is a specialized object that contains, manages, and provides access to services within a Symfony application. Every service within a Symfony application is defined, configured, and made available within the service container.

How does the service container work in Symfony?

When creating a service in Symfony, it is necessary to define the service in the application's service configuration file. This file is generally named `services.yaml` or `services.xml` within the `config` folder of the Symfony application. Inside this file, services can be defined and their dependencies configured.

For example, to define a service that handles sending emails, the service must be defined in the `services.yaml` file as follows:

```yaml
services:
    mailer_service:
        class: App\Service\MailerService
```

In this example, `mailer_service` is the name of the service that can be used to access the service within the application. `App\Service\MailerService` is the path to the class of the service that handles sending emails.

Once the service is defined in the service configuration file, it is possible to access the service within any part of the Symfony application using the service container. For instance, to access the `mailer_service` service, the following code can be used:

```php
$container->get('mailer_service');
```

In this case, `$container` is the service container object that provides access to services within the Symfony application. By calling the `get` method on the service container object with the service name as an argument, it is possible to retrieve the service instance and use it within the application.

What are the advantages of using services and the service container in Symfony?

The use of services and the service container in Symfony offers several significant advantages in terms of code structure, modularity, maintainability, and testability. Some of the key advantages are:

- Clear and modular: By defining services within the service container, it is possible to keep code well-structured, modularized, and easily understandable. Services can be separated into different files and organized based on the specific functionalities they perform, simplifying code management and maintenance.

- Reduction of code duplication: By using services in Symfony, it is possible to reduce code duplication within the application. Services can be reused in different parts of the application without having to repeat the same business logic multiple times, contributing to greater code coherence and consistency.

- Testability: Services in Symfony are designed to be easily testable. Thanks to the separation of responsibilities and clear definition of dependencies within the service container, individual services can be tested autonomously, ensuring that the code functions correctly and that any changes do not lead to unforeseen malfunctions.

- Dependency management: The service container in Symfony automatically manages dependencies between services within the application. When one service depends on another service, dependencies can be configured in the service configuration file, allowing the service container to automatically inject dependencies when the service is requested.

- Scalability: By using services in Symfony, it is possible to create a scalable architecture for the application. New services can be added or existing services modified without affecting the rest of the application, simplifying the update and expansion of the application over time.

Additionally, Symfony provides a range of advanced features for managing and configuring services within the application. For example, services can be defined as public or private services, dependencies can be configured with autowiring tools, and decorated services can be created to extend or modify the behavior of existing services.

Furthermore, Symfony provides extensive support for managing services through the command line with the Symfony Console bundle. Using the `debug:container` command, it is possible to view a list of all services defined in the service container and obtain detailed information about each service, including associated tags, aliases, and dependencies.

Services and the service container in Symfony are essential for developing robust, scalable, and testable applications. By using services in Symfony, it is possible to maintain code that is well-structured, modularized, and easily testable, allowing for greater code coherence, consistency, and flexibility in the application. Symfony makes it easy and intuitive to manage services within the application, providing a range of advanced features for configuring, managing, and testing services, ensuring that the application functions efficiently and reliably.

5. Routing in Symfony by Symfony

Symfony is a very popular and widely used open-source PHP framework for web application development. One of its main features is the flexible and powerful routing system that allows developers to easily manage user requests and route them to the correct controllers.

The routing system in Symfony is based on a centralized configuration file called "routes.yaml" or "routes.php" where it is defined how different URL requests should be handled. This configuration file can be organized hierarchically and modularly to ensure efficient route management and easy maintainability.

Routes in Symfony are defined using a set of rules that allow associating a specific URL with a controller and a method within the application. These rules can include any type of pattern to capture data from the URL and pass it to the controller dynamically.

For example, a simple route in Symfony could be defined as follows:

```yaml
hello:
    path: /hello
    controller: App\Controller\HelloController::index
```

In this case, when a user navigates to the address "/hello", the request will be sent to the "index" method of the "HelloController" controller. This allows developers to separate the application logic into distinct controllers and maintain better code organization.

Symfony also offers the ability to define parametric routes that allow capturing data from the URL and passing it to the controller as parameters. For example:

```yaml
user_profile:
    path: /user/{id}
    controller: App\Controller\UserController::profile
```

In this case, the URL "/user/123" will be associated with the "UserController" controller and the "profile" method, passing the value "123" as the "id" parameter. This is particularly useful for managing dynamic pages and customizing content based on user inputs.

Additionally, Symfony supports defining

routes with constraints to control the data passed as parameters. For example, it is possible to define a constraint to only accept numerical values as a parameter:

```yaml
route_with_constraint:
    path: /test/{id}
    controller: App\Controller\TestController::index
    requirements:
        id: \d+
```

In this way, the URL "/test/abc" will not match this route because it does not meet the numeric constraint imposed. This is useful to ensure that routes are properly matched and to prevent errors or security issues.

In case of complex routes or the need to handle different types of HTTP requests, Symfony offers the possibility to define nested routes, route groups, and prefixes to neatly organize all the routes in the application.

For example, it is possible to define a group of routes with a common prefix for all routes within a specific endpoint of the application:

```yaml
api_v1:
    path: /
    controller: App\Controller\ApiController::index
    prefix: /api/v1
    routes:
        - path: /users
          controller: App\Controller\UserController::index
```

```
  - path: /users/{id}
    controller: App\Controller\UserController::show
```

In this way, all routes within the "api_v1" group will have the prefix "/api/v1" and will follow the logic defined in the corresponding controller. This allows for better route organization and simplifies request management in the application.

Symfony also offers a powerful caching system for routes that improves application performance by storing in memory the mapping between URLs and controllers. This is particularly useful for reducing page loading times and optimizing server resources.

In summary, the routing system in Symfony is extremely flexible and powerful, allowing developers to easily manage user requests and route them to the correct controllers. With its simple YAML syntax and the ability to handle parametric routes, constraints, groups, and prefixes, Symfony provides an efficient way to define and organize routes within web applications.

In conclusion, Symfony is a versatile and comprehensive PHP framework that offers a wide range of features for developing web applications of any size and complexity. With its advanced and customizable routing system, Symfony enables developers to effectively manage user requests and create scalable, secure, and high-performance web applications.

6. Controllers, Actions, and Twig: Symfony's Template Engine

Symfony is a PHP framework that provides a wide range of functionalities for developing modern and complex web applications. Among Symfony's fundamental components are controllers, actions, and Twig, a template engine that facilitates the creation of dynamic and personalized web pages.

Controllers are PHP classes that handle HTTP requests and orchestrate the business logic of the application. Each controller is associated with one or more actions, which represent the methods of the class that are executed in response to a specific request. Actions are typically responsible for processing data, calling services or repositories, and preparing data to be passed to the template for rendering.

An example of a controller in Symfony could be the following:

```php
<?php

namespace App\Controller;

use Symfony\Bundle\FrameworkBundle\Controller\AbstractController;
use Symfony\Component\HttpFoundation\Response;
use Symfony\Component\Routing\Annotation\Route;

class BlogController extends AbstractController
```

```php
{
    /**
     * @Route("/blog", name="blog_list")
     */
    public function list(): Response
    {
        $posts = [
            ['title' => 'Post 1', 'content' => 'Lorem ipsum dolor sit amet'],
            ['title' => 'Post 2', 'content' => 'Consectetur adipiscing elit'],
        ];

        return $this->render('blog/list.html.twig', [
            'posts' => $posts,
        ]);
    }
```

```
}
```

In this example, the `BlogController` defines a `list()` action that handles the display of a list of posts on the blog. The `list()` function retrieves posts from the repository (in this case hard-coded for simplicity) and passes them to the `blog/list.html.twig` template for rendering.

Twig is Symfony's default template engine and provides a clear and intuitive syntax for creating dynamic and reusable HTML layouts. With Twig, you can define variables, loops, conditions, and blocks to manage the presentation logic of data in the template.

Here is an example of a Twig template for displaying the list of posts on the blog:

```twig
{# templates/blog/list.html.twig #}

{% extends 'base.html.twig' %}

{% block title %}Blog{% endblock %}

{% block body %}
    <h1>Blog</h1>

    <ul>
        {% for post in posts %}
            <li>
                <h2>{{ post.title }}</h2>
                <p>{{ post.content }}</p>
            </li>
        {% endfor %}
```

```
    </ul>

{% endblock %}
```

In this template, we use the `{% for %}` tag to iterate over the posts and display them in an unordered list. We also use the `{{ }}` syntax to interpolate variables within the template and display the title and content of each post.

Symfony automatically integrates Twig into the framework and offers advanced features such as including partial templates, template inheritance, and block management. Additionally, Symfony allows you to customize Twig configuration to handle custom extensions, filters, and Twig functions.

For example, we can extend the `base.html.twig` template to include the header and footer on all templates of our site:

```twig
{# templates/base.html.twig #}

<!DOCTYPE html>
<html>
<head>
    <title>{% block title %}{% endblock %} - My Blog</title>
</head>
<body>
    <header>
        <h1>My Blog</h1>
        <nav>
            <ul>
                <li><a href="{{ path('blog_list') }}">Home</a></li>
            </ul>
```

```
        </nav>
    </header>

    <main>
        {% block body %}{% endblock %}
    </main>

    <footer>
        &copy; 2021 My Blog
    </footer>
</body>
</html>
```

In this example, the `base.html.twig` template defines the basic structure of our site's layout, including the header with the blog title and navigation, the main content of the template, and the footer with the copyright.

By using template inheritance, we can define the specific content of each page by extending the base template and overriding the `{% block %}` blocks with the custom page content.

In conclusion, controllers, actions, and Twig are fundamental components of Symfony that facilitate the development of dynamic and personalized web applications. Controllers manage requests and orchestrate the application logic, actions process data and prepare information to be passed to the template for rendering, while Twig provides an intuitive and powerful template engine for creating dynamic and reusable HTML layouts. Symfony seamlessly integrates Twig into the framework and offers advanced functionalities for managing templates, including template inheritance, partial inclusion, and customization of Twig configuration.
Symfony is one of the most widely used and appreciated PHP frameworks in the developer community due to its versatility, high

performance, and ease of use, making it an ideal choice for developing complex and reliable web applications.

7. The View: template and layout and The View: helper Symfony

The View is one of the essential components in the Symfony framework, and plays a fundamental role in the process of rendering a web page. Symfony's View uses templates and layouts to define the structure and visual appearance of a page, while helpers are used to add extra functionality and simplify data management within the View.

The template is the file that defines the structure of a web page, and contains the HTML, CSS, and JavaScript code necessary to properly display the content. In Symfony, templates are usually stored in the "templates" directory within the project folder, and must have the ".html.twig" extension. Templates can include variables and conditions to make the content of the page dynamic, and can be extended or included in other templates to reuse code.

An example of a template in Symfony could be the following:

```twig
<!DOCTYPE html>
<html>
<head>
    <title>{{ page_title }}</title>
</head>
<body>
    <h1>{{ page_title }}</h1>

    <p>{{ page_content }}</p>

    <ul>
        {% for item in menu_items %}
```

```
        <li>{{ item }}</li>
      {% endfor %}
    </ul>
  </body>
</html>
```

In this example, the template contains variables such as "page_title", "page_content", and "menu_items" that will be dynamically populated within the Controller before being rendered. The "for" loop is used to iterate over the elements of the "menu_items" array and display them as an unordered list.

The layout is a concept similar to the template, but refers to the overall structure of the web page, including elements such as the header, footer, and sidebar. In Symfony, layouts are generally stored in the "templates/layouts" directory and can be extended by templates to define the general structure of the page. A typical layout could contain code similar to the following:

```twig
<!DOCTYPE html>
<html>
<head>
    <title>My Website</title>
</head>
<body>
    <header>
        <h1>My Website</h1>
    </header>

    <main>
        {% block content %} {% endblock %}
    </main>
```

```
    <footer>
        &copy; My Website
    </footer>
</body>
</html>
```

In this example, the layout defines a header with the site's title, a main block where the dynamic content of the templates will be inserted, and a footer with the site's copyright.

Helpers are pre-defined functions that can be used within templates to add extra functionality and simplify data management. Symfony provides a series of built-in helpers to perform common operations such as date handling, string manipulation, and number formatting. Helpers are usually called within templates using the "app" prefix.

For example, the "date" helper can be used to display the current date within a template:

```twig
<p>Today's date is: {{ app.date() }}</p>
```

The "truncate" helper can be used to limit the number of characters in a string:

```twig
<p>{{ app.truncate('Lorem ipsum dolor sit amet', 10) }}</p>
```

The "number_format" helper can be used to format a number with thousands separators and decimals:

```twig
<p>{{ app.number_format(12345.67, 2) }}</p>
```

These are just a few examples of how helpers can simplify data management within Symfony templates, and the framework offers a wide range of built-in helpers that can be used to perform a variety of operations.

In conclusion, the View in Symfony is a fundamental component for creating dynamic and interactive web pages, and uses templates, layouts, and helpers to define the structure and visual appearance of pages. Templates define the content and structure of a page, layouts define the overall structure of the page, while helpers add extra functionality and simplify data management. Through the combined use of templates, layouts, and helpers, it is possible to create complex and highly customizable web pages in Symfony.

8. The Model: Propel The data classes and The model: objects Symfony Criteria

Symfony is a very powerful and flexible open-source PHP framework that allows you to build web applications of any size and complexity. One of the fundamental components of Symfony is the Model: Propel, an ORM (Object-Relational Mapping) that allows you to manage and manipulate database data effectively and intuitively.

The Model: Propel is based on PHP Object Data Model (PODM) and offers a range of advanced features for data management, such as creating data models, CRUD operations (Create, Read, Update, Delete), handling relationships between database tables, and much more. Additionally, Propel supports various types of databases, including MySQL, PostgreSQL, SQLite, and Microsoft SQL Server, ensuring greater flexibility and scalability.

Data classes in Propel are represented by objects that correspond to the database tables. Each data class is properly mapped with the table fields and provides methods to access and manipulate data securely and consistently. For example, if you have a "users" table with fields "id," "username," and "email," you can create a User class representing a single record in that table.

Here is an example of how a data class in Propel might look like:

```php
// User.php

use Propel\Runtime\Map\TableMap;
use Propel\Runtime\ActiveQuery\ModelCriteria;
use Propel\Runtime\ActiveRecord\ActiveRecord;
```

```php
class User extends ActiveRecord
{
    protected $id;
    protected $username;
    protected $email;

    public function getId()
    {
        return $this->id;
    }

    public function getUsername()
    {
        return $this->username;
    }
```

```php
    public function getEmail()
    {
        return $this->email;
    }
}
```

In the example above, the User class represents a record in the "users" table with the fields "id," "username," and "email." Each field is represented by a protected property, and the class provides methods to access the data securely.

Criteria objects are another powerful feature of Propel that allows you to perform complex queries and filter data effectively. Criteria objects are essentially objects that contain a series of conditions and filters applied to queries to select desired data. For example, you can create a Criteria to select all users with a specific username or email.

Here is an example of how a Criteria might look like in Propel:

```php
// UserQuery.php

use Propel\Runtime\ActiveQuery\Criteria;
use Propel\Runtime\ActiveQuery\ModelCriteria;

class UserQuery extends ModelCriteria
{
    public function filterByUsername($username)
    {
        $this->filterBy('username', $username, Criteria::EQUAL);
```

```
        return $this;
    }


    public function filterByEmail($email)
    {
        $this->filterBy('email', $email, Criteria::EQUAL);
        return $this;
    }
}
```

In the example above, the UserQuery class extends ModelCriteria and provides methods to filter data based on username and email. These methods automatically create and apply criteria to the query to select the desired data.

Using Symfony with Propel is highly

advantageous as Symfony provides a range of components and functionalities that simplify web application development and enhance programmer productivity. For instance, Symfony offers a flexible routing system, a powerful templating system, a robust authentication and authorization system, and much more.

Here is an example of how you can use Symfony with Propel to create a simple web application:

1. Install Symfony Installer via Composer:

```
composer global require symfony/symfony-installer
```

2. Create a new Symfony project:

```
symfony new my_project_name
```

3. Install the Propel component via Composer:

```
composer require propel/propel
```

4. Configure Propel to use Symfony:

```
<?php

// app/config/config.yml
```

```
propel:
    database:
        connections:
            default:
                adapter: mysql
                dsn: 'mysql:host=localhost;dbname=my_database'
                user: my_username
                password: my_password
    generator:
        defaultConnection: default
```

5. Generate data classes and database model with Propel:

```
```

```
php bin/console propel:database:create
php bin/console propel:sql:build
php bin/console propel:sql:insert
php bin/console propel:model:build
```

6. Use Propel to access data in Symfony controller:

```php
// src/Controller/UserController.php

use Symfony\Bundle\FrameworkBundle\Controller\AbstractController;

class UserController extends AbstractController
{
```

```php
    public function index()
    {
        $users = UserQuery::create()->find();

        return $this->render('user/index.html.twig', [
            'users' => $users,
        ]);
    }
}
```

In this example, the UserController controller uses Propel to fetch all users from the database and passes them to the 'user/index.html.twig' template for display.

Using Symfony with Propel is a great choice for developing complex and scalable web applications. Symfony provides a range of components and functionalities that simplify the programmer's work, while Propel offers a powerful and flexible ORM for managing and manipulating database data efficiently. By combining these two technologies, you can create robust, high-performance, and easily maintainable web applications.

9. Symfony's Apps directory

Symfony is a PHP framework that provides a variety of tools and libraries for developing web applications efficiently and organized. One of the most useful features of Symfony is the Apps directory, which allows to organize all components of a Symfony project in a structured way.

The Apps directory is divided into several subdirectories, each with a specific role within the project. In this article, we will explore in detail the structure of Symfony's Apps directory and see how to best organize files and folders within it.

1. General structure of the Apps directory

Symfony's Apps directory is mainly divided into three main subdirectories:

- config: contains the application configuration files, such as routing configuration files, services configuration files, and environment variable files.

- src: contains the application source code, divided into bundles and bundle-less. Bundles are reusable libraries that contain specific functionalities of the application, while bundle-less files are source files that do not belong to a specific bundle.

- var: contains various files generated by the application, such as log files, cache files, and temporary files.

Each subdirectory can contain additional subdirectories and files, depending on the specific project needs. For example, additional folders can be created within the src directory to further organize the code in a more detailed way.

2. Subdirectories of the Apps directory

Now let's take a detailed look at the main subdirectories of the Apps directory:

- config: as mentioned before, the config directory contains the application configuration files. Some of the most important files in this folder include:

  - routes.yaml: the application's routing configuration file, which associates URLs with corresponding resources.

  - services.yaml: the application's services configuration file, which defines available services and their dependencies.

  - parameters.yaml: the application's environment variable configuration file, which allows defining dynamic values used within the code.

- src: the src directory contains the application source code. Inside this folder, you can find:

- AppBundle: a folder containing the source code of the main bundle of the application, which contains common functionalities for the entire project.

- Controller: a folder containing the application's controllers, which handle HTTP requests and return corresponding responses.

- Entity: a folder containing the application's entities, which represent database tables and are used to interact with data.

- Repository: a folder containing the application's repositories, which contain queries to retrieve and manipulate data from entities.

- Form: a folder containing the application's forms, which handle validation and management of data entered by users.

- Service: a folder containing the application's services, which contain business logic and reusable functionalities.

- var: the var directory contains files generated

by the application during execution. Some of the most important files in this folder are:

 - cache: a folder containing cache files generated by the application, which help improve performance by temporarily storing data.

 - log: a folder containing log files of the application, which record events and errors during execution.

 - tmp: a folder containing temporary files generated by the application, used to store temporary data.

3. Practical examples

To better understand how to best organize files and folders within the Apps directory of Symfony, let's consider some practical examples.

Let's say we have a Symfony project for

managing an online library. We will organize the Apps directory as follows:

- config:

  - routes.yaml: in the routing configuration file, we will define routes for managing books, authors, and categories.

  - services.yaml: in the services configuration file, we will define services for managing business logic.

  - parameters.yaml: in the environment variable configuration file, we will define API keys for integration with external services.

- src:

  - AppBundle:

    - Controller: in this folder, we will create controllers for handling HTTP requests, such as BookController, AuthorController, and CategoryController.

    - Entity: in this folder, we will create

entities to represent books, authors, and categories.

- Repository: in this folder, we will create repositories to manage data retrieval queries.

- Form: in this folder, we will create forms to manage user-entered data.

- Service: in this folder, we will create services for managing business logic, such as BookService, AuthorService, and CategoryService.

- var:

  - cache: in this folder, cache files will be generated to improve application performance.

  - log: in this folder, log files will be generated to record events and errors during execution.

  - tmp: in this folder, temporary files will be generated to store temporary data.

By organizing files and folders in this way, it will be easier to manage and maintain the project over time. Additionally, a well-organized structure helps make the code more readable and maintainable, facilitating teamwork.

Here is an example of the structure of an "apps" directory in a Symfony project:

Copy

```
apps/
    ├── app1/
    │   ├── cache/
    │   ├── config/
    │   ├── logs/
    │   ├── src/
    │   ├── web/
```

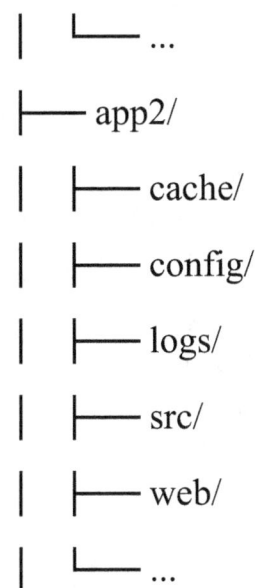

```
|   └── ...
├── app2/
|   ├── cache/
|   ├── config/
|   ├── logs/
|   ├── src/
|   ├── web/
|   └── ...
```

Each application (e.g. "app1" and "app2" in the example above) has its own "cache" folder to store cached data from requests, a "config" folder to contain configuration files, a "logs" folder for application logs, and a "src" folder for the application's source code. Additionally, there is usually a "web" folder containing publicly accessible files.

Furthermore, each application contains files such as the "kernel" that manages the basic logic of the application and "bundles" that are packages of reusable code within the application.

Symfony's Apps directory is a useful resource for structuring all components of a Symfony project in an organized manner. By leveraging the available subdirectories and following good organizational practices, it is possible to create robust and high-performing web applications with Symfony.

10. Creating Symfony Libraries

Symfony is one of the most popular and powerful PHP frameworks available today. Thanks to its modular and flexible architecture, Symfony offers developers the ability to quickly and efficiently create complex and scalable web applications. One of the most important aspects of Symfony is library management, which allows developers to organize their code in a structured and reusable way.

In this article, I will show you how to create and use Symfony libraries in practice, with a practical example that will guide you step by step through the process of creating and integrating a custom library.

Creating a Symfony Library

To create a Symfony library, you need to

follow a series of steps that will allow you to organize your code efficiently and in a reusable manner. Here are the main steps:

1. **Creating a directory structure**: First and foremost, you need to create a directory structure for your library. This directory structure should include at least a `composer.json` file to define your library's dependencies and an `src` directory for the library's source code.

2. **Defining dependencies**: In the `composer.json` file, you need to define your library's dependencies. Dependencies are other PHP libraries or packages that your library uses. You can define dependencies like this:

```json
{
  "require": {
```

```
        "symfony/routing": "^v5.3",
        "symfony/http-foundation": "^v5.3"
    }
}
```

In this example, our library depends on Symfony's `routing` and `http-foundation` libraries.

3. **Creating source code**: Now it's time to create the source code for your library. This source code should be organized in the `src` directory and should include at least one or more PHP files that define the classes and functions of your library.

For example, let's say we want to create a library that handles HTTP requests easily and intuitively. Our source code could include a `RequestHandler` class that defines methods to handle HTTP requests:

```php
<?php

namespace MyLibrary;

use Symfony\Component\HttpFoundation\Request;

class RequestHandler
{
    public function handleRequest(Request $request)
    {
        // Code to handle the HTTP request
    }
```

}
```

4. **Defining the namespace**: It is important to define a namespace for your source code, to avoid conflicts with other libraries. The namespace should correspond to the directory structure of your library. In our example, we defined the namespace as `MyLibrary`.

5. **Registering the autoloader**: To automatically load your library's classes without having to manually include each file, you need to register an autoloader. You can do this by adding the following code to your `composer.json` file:

```json
{
    "autoload": {

```
        "psr-4": {
            "MyLibrary\\": "src/"
        }
    }
}
```

This way, Composer will automatically load all classes under the `MyLibrary` namespace from the `src` directory when they are requested.

6. **Publishing the library**: Now that you have created your library, you can publish it on GitHub or Packagist (the official PHP library repository). This way, other developers can use your library in their applications.

Using a Symfony Library in a Project

Once you have created and published your Symfony library, you can use it in an existing Symfony project. Here's how you can do it:

1. **Installing the library**: To use your library in a Symfony project, you need to add its dependency to the project's `composer.json` file. You can do this by adding the following code:

```json
{
    "require": {
        "my/library": "^1.0"
    }
}
```

This way, Composer will automatically install your library when you run the `composer install` command.

2. **Using the library**: Once your library is installed, you can use it in your project's code. For example, if you want to use the `RequestHandler` class from your library, you can do so like this:

```php
<?php

use MyLibrary\RequestHandler;

$requestHandler = new RequestHandler();
$request = ...; // Creating a Request object
$requestHandler->handleRequest($request);
```

This way, your Symfony library will be

integrated into your project and you can use it to handle HTTP requests easily and intuitively.

Practical Example

To conclude, I will show you a practical example of creating and using a Symfony library that handles HTTP requests. Follow the steps listed above to create your library and use it in an existing Symfony project.

1. **Directory structure**:

```
my-library/
├── src/
│   └── RequestHandler.php
├── composer.json
```

```

2. **Defining dependencies**:

```json
{
  "require": {
    "symfony/http-foundation": "^v5.3"
  }
}
```

3. **Library source code**:

```php
// src/RequestHandler.php
```
```

```php
<?php

namespace MyLibrary;

use Symfony\Component\HttpFoundation\Request;

class RequestHandler
{
    public function handleRequest(Request $request)
    {
        // Code to handle the HTTP request
    }
}
```

4. **Defining the namespace**:

```php
namespace MyLibrary;
```

5. **Registering the autoloader**:

```json
{
    "autoload": {
        "psr-4": {
            "MyLibrary\\": "src/"
        }
    }
}
```

6. **Using the library in the Symfony project**:

```php
<?php

use MyLibrary\RequestHandler;
use Symfony\Component\HttpFoundation\Request;

$requestHandler = new RequestHandler();
$request = Request::createFromGlobals();
$requestHandler->handleRequest($request);
```

In this practical example, we have created a Symfony library that handles HTTP requests easily and intuitively. We defined a `RequestHandler` class that defines a `handleRequest` method to handle HTTP requests and used it in an existing Symfony project to handle an HTTP request created using Symfony's `Request` class.

Conclusion

In this article, I showed you how to create and use Symfony libraries in practice, with a practical example that guided you step by step through the process of creating and integrating a custom library. Symfony libraries are a powerful tool that allows you to organize your code efficiently and in a reusable way, enabling you to create complex and scalable web applications quickly and efficiently. I hope this article has been helpful and has inspired you to make the most of Symfony's capabilities in creating your web applications.

11. Creating the database in Symfony

Symfony is a very popular open-source PHP framework widely used for web application development. One of its most appreciated features is its Doctrine component, which provides a comprehensive ORM (Object Relational Mapping) for database management. In this article, we will see how to create and manage a database in Symfony using Doctrine.

Before we begin, make sure you have Symfony installed in your development environment. If you haven't done so already, you can follow the detailed instructions available on Symfony's official documentation.

Once Symfony is installed, you can create a new project using the `symfony new project_name` command. After creating the project, navigate to your project directory and start working on the database.

Creating a new entity

In Symfony, an entity represents a database table. You can create a new entity using the `make:entity` command. For example, if you want to create an entity to manage users on your site, you can run the following command:

```bash
php bin/console make:entity User
```

This command will guide you through the entity creation process, prompting you to specify the different fields you want to include. For instance, for a User entity, you may have fields such as `username`, `email`, and `password`. Once you have specified the fields, the command will automatically generate a new PHP class corresponding to the entity in the `src/Entity/User.php` path.

Defining entity properties

Within the generated User.php class, you will find the definitions of the fields you specified during the entity creation. For example, you may have something like this:

```php
<?php

namespace App\Entity;

use Doctrine\ORM\Mapping as ORM;

/**
 *
 @ORM\Entity(repositoryClass="App\Reposit
```

ory\UserRepository")
 */
class User
{
    /**
     * @ORM\Id()
     * @ORM\GeneratedValue()
     * @ORM\Column(type="integer")
     */
    private $id;

    /**
     * @ORM\Column(type="string", length=255)
     */
    private $username;

```
    /**
     * @ORM\Column(type="string", length=255)
     */
    private $email;

    /**
     * @ORM\Column(type="string", length=255)
     */
    private $password;

    // ...other fields and methods
}
```

In the User class, each field is defined as a property of the class with Doctrine annotations specifying the entity's mapping details with the database. For example, the `@ORM\Column` annotation is used to specify the type and length of the field in the database.

Database migration

After defining the entities in your Symfony project, you need to create the corresponding tables in the database through a migration. To create and apply the migration, you can use the `doctrine:migrations:diff` command followed by the `doctrine:migrations:migrate` command.

```bash
php bin/console doctrine:migrations:diff
php bin/console doctrine:migrations:migrate
```

The first command `doctrine:migrations:diff` generates a migration file based on the changes made to the entities compared to the existing database structure. The second command `doctrine:migrations:migrate` effectively applies the migration, creating or updating the tables in the database.

Data management in the database

Once the tables are created in the database, you can start managing data using Symfony and Doctrine. You can create, read, update, and delete records from the database using the entity repository and EntityManager functions provided by Doctrine.

For example, to insert a new record into the `User` table, you can do the following:

```php
<?php

use App\Entity\User;
```

```
$user = new User();
$user->setUsername('john_doe');
$user->setEmail('john@example.com');
$user->setPassword('password123');

$entityManager->persist($user);
$entityManager->flush();
```

In this code snippet, we created a new instance of the `User` class, set the field values, and saved the record in the database using the `persist` method of EntityManager and the `flush` method to actually perform the insert operation in the database.

Database querying

You can perform complex queries in the

database using Doctrine Query Language (DQL) or Doctrine's QueryBuilder. For example, if you want to select all users with an email ending in '@example.com', you can write a DQL query like this:

```php
<?php

use App\Entity\User;

$users = $entityManager->createQuery(
    'SELECT u
    FROM App\Entity\User u
    WHERE u.email LIKE :emailPattern'
)->setParameter('emailPattern', '%@example.com')
->getResult();
```

In this example, we created a DQL query that selects all users whose email field ends with '@example.com' using the `createQuery` method of EntityManager. We also used the `setParameter` method to pass a parameter to the query and then fetch the results using the `getResult` method.

Conclusion

In this article, we have seen how to create and manage a database in Symfony using Doctrine, the ORM component included in the framework. We have learned how to define entities, create migrations, manage data in the database, and perform complex queries using Symfony and Doctrine.

Symfony and Doctrine provide a powerful combination for working with databases in a simple and efficient manner. By using the features provided by Doctrine, you can handle data persistence in your Symfony project quickly and cleanly.

Thanks to its flexibility and numerous features, Symfony is an excellent choice for developing complex and scalable web applications that require a robust and well-structured database. With an ORM-driven approach like Doctrine, you can focus on developing your applications without having to manually manage low-level database operations.

12. Creating modules in Symfony

Symfony is a very popular open-source PHP framework that allows developers to create robust, scalable, and high-performing web applications. One key aspect of Symfony is its modular architecture, which allows developers to organize code efficiently and in a reusable manner, thus improving the maintainability and scalability of applications.

Modules in Symfony are a fundamental part of the application structure and allow for organizing code into distinct functional units, each performing a specific task. Modules can contain controllers, views, models, services, and other application components, enabling developers to maintain a well-organized and separate structure.

Creating modules in Symfony is a relatively straightforward process, but it requires a certain familiarity with the framework and its fundamental concepts. In this article, we will explore how to create modules in Symfony and provide a practical example to illustrate the process.

Steps for creating modules in Symfony:

1. Create a new bundle: In Symfony, modules are commonly called "bundles" and are created using the `bin/console make:bundle` command. This command will automatically generate the basic structure of the bundle, including configuration files, basic controllers, and other necessary resources.

2. Define routes: One of the main features of modules in Symfony is defining routes, which allow associating controllers with application URLs. Routes can be defined in the `config/routes.yml` file of the bundle using YAML syntax.

3. Create controllers: Controllers are responsible for processing HTTP requests and generating corresponding responses. Controllers can be created within the bundle using the `bin/console make:controller` command and implementing the necessary business logic.

4. Create views: Views are template files used to display data to the user. Views can be created within the `templates` directory of the bundle and Twig can be used as the template engine to generate HTML output.

5. Create models: Models are responsible for interacting with the database or other data sources and providing data needed by the controllers. Models can be created within the `Entity` or `Repository` directory of the bundle, using Doctrine as the ORM to manage database operations.

Practical example of creating a module in

Symfony:

Suppose we want to create a module to manage products in an online store. We follow the steps described above to create our bundle dedicated to products.

1. Create a new bundle: we use the `bin/console make:bundle` command to create a new bundle called `ProductBundle`. This command will automatically generate the basic structure of the bundle, including configuration files, basic controllers, and other necessary resources.

2. Define routes: we define routes in the `config/routes.yml` file of the bundle to handle CRUD operations on products. For example, we define the following routes:

```yaml
```

```yaml
product_index:
    path: /products
    controller: ProductController::index

product_create:
    path: /products/create
    controller: ProductController::create

product_edit:
    path: /products/{id}/edit
    controller: ProductController::edit

product_delete:
    path: /products/{id}/delete
    controller: ProductController::delete
```

3. Create controllers: we create the `ProductController` within the bundle and implement the `index`, `create`, `edit`, and `delete` methods to handle CRUD operations on products.

```php
namespace App\ProductBundle\Controller;

use Symfony\Bundle\FrameworkBundle\Controller\AbstractController;
use Symfony\Component\HttpFoundation\Response;
use Symfony\Component\Routing\Annotation\Route;

class ProductController extends AbstractController
```

```php
{
    /**
     * @Route("/products", name="product_index")
     */
    public function index(): Response
    {
        // Logic to display the list of products
    }

    /**
     * @Route("/products/create", name="product_create")
     */
    public function create(): Response
    {
        // Logic to create a new product
    }
```

```php
/**
 * @Route("/products/{id}/edit", name="product_edit")
 */
public function edit($id): Response
{
    // Logic to edit an existing product
}


/**
 * @Route("/products/{id}/delete", name="product_delete")
 */
public function delete($id): Response
{
    // Logic to delete an existing product
}
```

}
```

4. Create views: we create HTML template files within the `templates` directory of the bundle to display product data to the user. We use Twig as the template engine to generate HTML output.

5. Create models: we create the `Product` and `ProductRepository` models within the `Entity` and `Repository` directories of the bundle to manage product data. We use Doctrine as the ORM to interact with the database and provide data needed by the controllers.

```php
namespace App\ProductBundle\Entity;

use Doctrine\ORM\Mapping as ORM;

```
/**
 *
 * @ORM\Entity(repositoryClass="App\ProductBundle\Repository\ProductRepository")
 */
class Product
{
    // Define properties and methods of the Product model
}
```

```php
namespace App\ProductBundle\Repository;

use Doctrine\Bundle\DoctrineBundle\Repository\ServiceEntityRepository;
```

```php
use Doctrine\Persistence\ManagerRegistry;
use App\ProductBundle\Entity\Product;

class ProductRepository extends ServiceEntityRepository
{
    public function __construct(ManagerRegistry $registry)
    {
        parent::__construct($registry, Product::class);
    }

    // Define repository methods for database operations
}
```

With these steps, we have successfully created

a module to manage products in Symfony using a dedicated bundle. This allows us to maintain a well-organized and separate structure within the application, improving code maintainability and scalability.

In conclusion, creating modules in Symfony is a fundamental process for efficiently organizing and structuring the code of web applications. Modules allow developers to separate different functionalities of the application into distinct and reusable units, facilitating code development and maintenance. With the guidance and practical example provided in this article, we hope to have helped you better understand how to create modules in Symfony and how to use them in your next project.

13. Symfony Bundle

Symfony comes with many built-in features, but sometimes you may need to extend its functionality with Symfony bundles. Bundles are software packages that provide additional functionality and can be easily integrated into your Symfony project. In this article, we will explore what Symfony bundles are, how to install and use them in your Symfony project, and provide some examples of popular bundles.

What is a Symfony bundle?

A Symfony bundle is a software package that contains a series of files and directories that provide additional functionality to a Symfony application. Bundles can include everything from PHP classes and Twig templates to YAML configurations and CSS files.

Symfony bundles are designed to be modular and reusable, which means that you can easily add, remove, and configure bundles within your Symfony project. Symfony bundles are often used to add common functionalities such as user authentication, integration with external APIs, and implementation of industry-specific features.

How to install a Symfony bundle?

To install a Symfony bundle in your project, you need to add the bundle package to your composer.json file and then run the composer update command to install the package. After installing the bundle, you need to register the bundle in the AppKernel.php file of your Symfony project.

For example, let's say you want to install the FOSUserBundle, which provides user management functionalities. To install the FOSUserBundle, you can add the following code to your composer.json file:

```json
"require": {
    "friendsofsymfony/user-bundle": "~2.0"
}
```

After adding the bundle package to your composer.json file, you can run the following composer command to install the package:

```bash
composer update
```

Once the bundle is installed, you need to register the bundle in the AppKernel.php file of your Symfony project. To do so, add the following code to your AppKernel.php file:

```php
public function registerBundles()
{
    $bundles = array(
        // ...
        new FOS\UserBundle\FOSUserBundle(),
    );
    // ...
}
```

After registering the bundle in your AppKernel.php file, the bundle will be available for use in your Symfony project.

How to use a Symfony bundle?

Once you have installed a Symfony bundle in your project, you can use the bundle's functionalities by adding its configurations to your Symfony configuration file (usually a YAML configuration file).

For example, suppose you have installed the SonataAdminBundle, which provides an admin interface for your Symfony project. To use the SonataAdminBundle, you need to add its configurations to your Symfony configuration file.

Here is an example configuration for the SonataAdminBundle:

```yaml
sonata_admin:
    title: Admin Panel
    class:
```

```
user: AppBundle\Entity\User
post: AppBundle\Entity\Post
```

After adding the bundle's configurations to your Symfony configuration file, you can start using the bundle's functionalities in your project. For example, you can easily create an admin panel for the entities defined in the configuration file.

Popular Symfony bundles

There are many Symfony bundles available that provide a wide range of functionalities. Here are some popular bundles that you may find useful for your Symfony project:

1. FOSUserBundle: provides user management functionalities such as registration, login, and password reset.

2. SonataAdminBundle: provides an admin interface for your Symfony project, allowing you to manage database entities.

3. KnpPaginatorBundle: provides pagination functionalities for tables and lists in your Symfony project.

4. VichUploaderBundle: provides file upload functionalities for your Symfony project, allowing you to handle file upload and storage.

5. StofDoctrineExtensionsBundle: provides additional functionalities for Doctrine, such as Doctrine extensions and custom field types.

These are just a few examples of popular Symfony bundles available. You can explore the Symfony Flex Marketplace to find other available Symfony bundles and use those that best fit your project needs.

Conclusion

Symfony bundles are an essential part of developing Symfony projects, allowing you to easily extend the framework's functionality and add new features to your project. With a wide range of bundles available, you can easily find and use bundles that best fit your project's needs.

Throughout this article, we have looked at what Symfony bundles are, how to install and use them in your Symfony project, and provided some examples of popular bundles. We hope this article has helped you better understand the importance and usage of Symfony bundles in your Symfony project.

14. Symfony Console from Symfony Dependency management with Composer Debugging Symfony applications Error and log management

Symfony Console is an advanced tool in Symfony that allows creating powerful command-line applications. With it, you can define custom commands that perform specific operations within the Symfony application. This tool is particularly useful for automating complex tasks and interacting with the application without the need for a user interface.

To create a command with Symfony Console, you need to create a class that extends Symfony's Command class and implement the configure() method to define the name and description of the command, as well as the execute() method to define the logic of the command itself. For example, a command to perform a calculation operation could be defined as follows:

```php
use Symfony\Component\Console\Command\Command;

use Symfony\Component\Console\Input\InputInterface;

use Symfony\Component\Console\Output\OutputInterface;

class CalculateCommand extends Command
{
    protected static $defaultName = 'app:calculate';

    protected function configure()
    {
        $this->setDescription('Perform a
```

```
calculation');
    }


    protected function execute(InputInterface $input, OutputInterface $output)
    {
        // Calculation command logic
        $output->writeln('Calculation performed successfully');
    }
}
```

Once the command is defined, you can register it in the src/Command/console.php file of the Symfony application to make it available from the command line. For example, to register the app:calculate command, you can do the following:

```php
use Symfony\Component\Console\Application;

require __DIR__.'/../vendor/autoload.php';
require __DIR__.'/../src/Command/CalculateCommand.php';

$application = new Application();
$application->add(new CalculateCommand());
$application->run();
```

With Composer, the PHP dependency manager, you can install and manage third-party libraries within a Symfony project. Composer uses a composer.json file to define the project's dependencies and a composer.lock file to store the specific versions of installed libraries. For example, to install the Symfony HttpClient library, you can run the command:

```bash
composer require symfony/http-client
```

By doing so, Composer will install the Symfony HttpClient library and all its dependencies in the Symfony project. Additionally, Composer takes care of managing library versions to ensure that dependencies are compatible with each other.

Debugging a Symfony application can be done using Symfony's built-in debugger or an external debugger like Xdebug. Symfony's debugger allows you to view detailed information about HTTP requests and responses, as well as SQL queries executed by the Doctrine ORM.

To activate Symfony's debugger, you can enable debug mode in the app_kernel.php of the Symfony project. For example, to enable the debugger in the development environment, you can do the following:

```php
if (in_array($this->getEnvironment(), array('dev', 'test'))) {

    $this->register(new Symfony\Bundle\DebugBundle\DebugBundle());

    $this->register(new Symfony\Bundle\WebProfilerBundle\WebProfilerBundle());

}
```

Once Symfony's debugger is enabled, you can view detailed debug information within the browser at the /_profiler path. This tool is particularly useful for identifying and resolving errors within the Symfony application.

Error and log management in Symfony can be done using the integrated Monolog component. Monolog is a powerful logging system that allows logging messages in various formats and severity levels. For example, to log an "error" type log message, you can do the following:

```php
use Symfony\Component\DependencyInjection\ContainerInterface;
use Psr\Log\LoggerInterface;

class MyService
{
    private $logger;

    public function __construct(LoggerInterface $logger)
```

```
    {
        $this->logger = $logger;
    }

    public function doSomething()
    {
        try {
            // Service logic
        } catch (Exception $e) {
            $this->logger->error('An error occurred: ' . $e->getMessage());
        }
    }
}
```

In this example, the MyService service receives an instance of the Monolog logger through dependency injection and logs an "error" type log message in case of an exception. Log messages logged by Monolog can be configured to be sent to different channels, such as log files, console, or remote log servers.

In conclusion, Symfony Console, Composer, Symfony's debugger, and Monolog are advanced tools that allow for efficient and professional development and management of Symfony applications. Using these tools can improve developer productivity, facilitate debugging and error management, and ensure a better experience for end users.

15.Creation of administration in Symfony

Symfony is a powerful open-source PHP framework widely used for developing modern and complex web applications. One of its distinctive features is the standardized and component-based architecture, which allows developers to easily create and manage a web application efficiently and scalably.

A fundamental part of every Symfony application is the administration, which handles all CRUD (Create, Read, Update, Delete) operations on the application's data. Symfony provides an integrated tool called Symfony MakerBundle, which greatly simplifies the process of creating an administration section to manage database data.

To create the administration in Symfony, it is necessary to follow a series of key steps. Initially, it is important to ensure that you have a working Symfony project already configured and a database with at least one data table to manage. Once these requirements are met, you can start creating the administration.

The first step is to install Symfony MakerBundle in the project using Composer, by running the following command in the terminal:

```
composer require symfony/maker-bundle --dev
```

This command will install the bundle in the `Maker` namespace and enable the bundle's creation tools.

Next, you can use the `make:admin:crud`

maker to automatically generate all the necessary logic for the administration of a specific entity. For example, if we have a `Product` entity, we can generate the administration for it with the following command:

```
php bin/console make:admin:crud --entity=Product
```

This command will automatically create all the necessary files for the administration of `Product`, including controllers, forms, templates, and routing.

Once the files are generated, you can review and customize the administration according to your needs. For example, you can modify displayed fields, add virtual calculated fields, apply custom filters, and more.

To make the administration accessible from the application, you need to add routes in the `config/routes.yaml` file, for example:

```
admin_product:
    path: '/admin/product'
    controller: App\Controller\Admin\ProductController::index
```

Finally, it is always advisable to run the command `php bin/console cache:clear` to clear any caches and reload the application with the new changes made.

Furthermore, Symfony provides additional features and advanced tools to manage the administration more effectively. For example, you can use the `Security` component to manage user authentication and assign roles and permissions to users to restrict access to the administration.

Another powerful feature of Symfony is the Symfony console, which provides a command-line interface to run Symfony commands and automate tasks. For example, you can use the Symfony console to generate code automatically, run database migrations, develop and test the application, and much more.

Moreover, Symfony offers excellent documentation and a vast community of active developers who share knowledge, best practices, and useful resources for development with Symfony. This makes it easier for developers to learn and use Symfony to create advanced and high-quality web applications.

In conclusion, creating and managing the administration in Symfony is a simple and efficient process thanks to the integrated tools and standardized conventions offered by the framework. By following the steps described above and leveraging Symfony's advanced features, you can easily create a complete and customized administration interface to manage application data with ease. Symfony is therefore an excellent choice for developing complex and scalable web applications with high productivity and quality.

16. Modifying Symfony's CSS and Layout

A key feature of Symfony is the adoption of the Model-View-Controller (MVC) design pattern, which helps developers separate business logic from presentation. Additionally, Symfony offers numerous tools and components to facilitate development and improve code maintainability.

One important aspect of any web application is the layout and visual style. Symfony allows developers to manage the layout and style of their applications using CSS style files. Modifying Symfony's CSS and layout is essential for creating a pleasant and intuitive user experience. In this article, we will look at how to modify Symfony's CSS and layout to customize the appearance of your application.

Before starting to modify Symfony's CSS and layout, it is important to understand how Symfony handles CSS style files. Symfony uses the Assetic component to manage CSS files and other assets like JavaScript and images. Assetic allows developers to organize and manage style files within the Symfony application.

To add a CSS file to your Symfony application, you can use the following code in the Twig layout file:

```twig
{% block stylesheets %}
    {% stylesheets filter='cssrewrite'
        'bundles/app/css/styles.css'
    %}
        <link rel="stylesheet" href="{{ asset_url }}" />
    {% endstylesheets %}
{% endblock %}
```

In this example, we are including the CSS file "styles.css" located in the "bundles/app/css/" folder within the "stylesheets" block of our Twig layout. The "{% stylesheets %}" statement from Assetic creates a single CSS file from all listed CSS files and caches it for improved performance.

In addition to including CSS files, Symfony also allows defining CSS styles directly in the Twig layout using the "style" tag. For example, in the main block of your Twig layout, you can insert inline CSS styles like the following:

```twig
{% block main %}

    <div style="background-color: #f2f2f2; padding: 10px;">

        <h1 style="color: #333;">Hello, Symfony!</h1>
```

```
    <p style="font-size: 16px; line-height: 1.5;">Welcome to your Symfony application.</p>

  </div>

{% endblock %}
```

This is useful when you want to apply specific CSS styles only to a certain section of the layout.

To modify Symfony's CSS, you can use different methods. One option is to override default CSS rules with new rules in a custom CSS file. For example, if you want to change the text color of h1 headers throughout your site, you can add this rule to your custom CSS file:

```css
h1 {
```

    color: #ff0000;

}
```

This way, every h1 header will be displayed in red instead of the default color.

Another way to modify Symfony's CSS is to use CSS variables. Symfony allows defining CSS variables within the "parameters.yml" file and using them in style files. For example, you can define a variable for the main site color in the "parameters.yml" file like this:

```yaml
# app/config/parameters.yml

parameters:

    primary_color: #3366ff;
```
```

Later, you can use this variable in CSS style files like this:

```css
.header {
    background-color: %primary_color%;
}
```

This way, you can centralize style definitions within the "parameters.yml" file and easily change the site's appearance by modifying the value of the primary variable.

Symfony also offers the possibility to use Sass (Syntactically Awesome Stylesheets) for defining style sheets. Sass adds advanced features to CSS style sheets such as variables, mixins, inheritance, and more. To use Sass in

Symfony, you need to install the Symfony Flex package and the Assetic component for Sass.

Once installed, you can create Sass files within the "assets" folder of the Symfony project. For example, you can create a "styles.scss" file and define variables, mixins, and CSS rules like this:

```scss
$primary-color: #3366ff;

.header {
    background-color: $primary-color;
}

.button {
    background-color: darken($primary-color, 10%);
```

    color: white;

    padding: 10px 20px;

}
```

Symfony will automatically compile Sass files into regular CSS files when the application is updated or loaded. This allows you to use Sass's advanced features to create style sheets that are easier to manage and maintain.

In addition to modifying CSS, you can customize Symfony's layout using Twig templates to define the page structure. A typical Symfony layout uses a base layout that includes common sections like the header, navigation menu, and footer. You can use Twig blocks to override common sections based on the currently viewed page.

For example, the base layout of a Symfony
```

application could be defined in a Twig file named "base.html.twig" as follows:

```twig
<!DOCTYPE html>
<html>
<head>
    <title>{% block title %}Welcome to Symfony{% endblock %}</title>
    {% block stylesheets %}{% endblock %}
</head>
<body>
  <header>
    {% block header %}
      <h1>Welcome to Symfony</h1>
    {% endblock %}
  </header>
```

```html
<nav>
    {% block navigation %}
    <ul>
        <li><a href="/">Home</a></li>
        <li><a href="/about">About</a></li>
        <li><a href="/contact">Contact</a></li>
    </ul>
    {% endblock %}
</nav>

<main>
    {% block body %} {% endblock %}
</main>

<footer>
```

```
    {% block footer %}
        &copy; 2021 Symfony
    {% endblock %}
  </footer>
 </body>
</html>
```

In this basic layout, we have defined blocks for the title, stylesheets, header, navigation, body, and footer of the page. Blocks can be overridden in specific page templates to customize the content and structure of the page.

For example, if you want to create a contact page with a different header and content, you can create a separate Twig template called "contact.html.twig" and override the desired blocks as shown below:

```twig
{% extends 'base.html.twig' %}

{% block title %}Contact Us{% endblock %}

{% block header %}
    <h1>Contact Us</h1>
{% endblock %}

{% block body %}
    <p>Feel free to contact us for any questions or inquiries.</p>
{% endblock %}
```

By using Twig templates and blocks, you can create a dynamic and flexible layout for your Symfony application pages. Additionally, Symfony offers advanced features such as routing and event handling that allow for further customization of the layout and behavior of the application.

In conclusion, customizing CSS and layout in Symfony is essential for creating a unique and satisfying user experience. Symfony offers numerous options for modifying CSS and defining page layouts using style sheets, CSS variables, Sass, and Twig templates. By utilizing these features, you can create a professional and well-designed web application with a personalized and consistent appearance.

17. HTTP Requests Management Response and Rendering in Symfony

Symfony is a widely used PHP framework for developing high-quality web applications. One crucial aspect of managing HTTP requests in Symfony is the ability to respond to users' requests effectively and efficiently.

Symfony offers a very flexible way to handle HTTP requests and generate custom responses to users. This is made possible through a series of components and features integrated into the framework.

When a user sends an HTTP request to the server, Symfony automatically handles the request, parses it, and routes it to the appropriate controller. The controller is the component that handles the business logic and generates the response to the user's request.

Once the controller has processed the request, it can generate a response using a variety of methods. For example, the controller can return a Symfony Response object that represents the HTTP response to be sent to the user. This Response object can contain plain text, HTML, JSON, or any other type of data to be displayed to the user.

Here is an example of how a controller in Symfony can generate a text response:

```php
use Symfony\Component\HttpFoundation\Response;

public function helloAction()
{
    return new Response('Hello, world!');
}
```

```

In this example, the `helloAction` method returns a Response object containing the text "Hello, world!". When a user accesses this page, they will simply see the message "Hello, world!".

Symfony also offers the ability to generate responses based on HTML templates. This can be useful when you want to display dynamic data to users. Symfony uses the Twig template engine to generate dynamic HTML pages.

Here is an example of how a controller can render an HTML template with dynamic data:

```php
use Symfony\Bundle\FrameworkBundle\Controlle

```
r\AbstractController;

use Symfony\Component\HttpFoundation\Response;

public function helloAction()
{
    $name = 'John';

    return $this->render('hello.html.twig', [
        'name' => $name
    ]);
}
```

In this example, the controller passes the name "John" as dynamic data to the 'hello.html.twig' HTML template rendering function. The Twig template can then access the data passed by the controller and render the HTML page based on it.

This is how the 'hello.html.twig' template file could look like:

```html
<!DOCTYPE html>
<html>
<head>
    <title>Welcome</title>
</head>
<body>
    <h1>Hello, {{ name }}!</h1>
</body>
</html>
```

When a user accesses the page generated by this controller, they will see the message "Hello, John!". The Twig template replaces the `name` variable with the value passed by the controller.

Symfony also offers the ability to generate JSON responses to users' requests. This is useful when you want to return structured data to users, for example in response to an AJAX request.

Here is an example of how a controller can generate a JSON response:

```php
use Symfony\Component\HttpFoundation\JsonResponse;

public function apiAction()
```

```
{
    $data = [
        'name' => 'John',
        'age' => 30
    ];

    return new JsonResponse($data);
}
```

In this example, the controller returns a JsonResponse object with the structured data contained in the array.

18. Using Validation Forms in Symfony

Symfony is an open-source PHP framework that offers developers a wide range of features for creating sophisticated and high-quality web applications. One of Symfony's most powerful features is its form management system, which allows developers to easily create and validate data input forms.

Using forms in Symfony is essential for creating interactive and dynamic user interfaces. Forms allow users to input and submit data through a web page, such as contact information, order details, or comments on an article.

To create a form in Symfony, you need to define a form model that describes the input fields and validation rules associated with each field. This model can be defined using Symfony's FormType class, which allows you to define form fields and validation rules declaratively.

For example, if you want to create a form to collect contact information, you can define a form model using the Symfony FormType class as follows:

```php
use Symfony\Component\Form\AbstractType;
use Symfony\Component\Form\FormBuilderInterface;

class ContactFormType extends AbstractType
{
    public function buildForm(FormBuilderInterface $builder, array $options)
    {
        $builder
```

```
            ->add('name')
            ->add('email')
            ->add('message');
    }
}
```

In this example, the ContactFormType form model defines three input fields: name, email, and message. Once the form model is defined, you can use it to create an instance of a form in a Symfony controller and render it on a web page.

```php
use Symfony\Component\HttpFoundation\Request;


public function contactAction(Request
```

```php
$request)
{
    $form = $this->createForm(ContactFormType::class);

    $form->handleRequest($request);

    if ($form->isSubmitted() && $form->isValid()) {
        // Form data is valid, handle form submission
    }

    return $this->render('contact.html.twig', [
        'form' => $form->createView(),
    ]);
}
```

In this example, the contactAction controller creates an instance of a form using the ContactFormType form model and handles it using the handleRequest() method. The handleRequest() method takes a Symfony Request object as a parameter and populates the form with user input data.

Once the form is handled, you can check if the form has been submitted and if the form data is valid using the isSubmitted() and isValid() methods. If the form has been submitted and the data is valid, you can process the form submission, such as saving the data to the database or sending a confirmation email.

One of the most powerful features of Symfony forms is the integrated form validation system, which allows developers to define custom validation rules for form input fields. Validation rules can be defined using annotations in the form data model or using the Symfony validation component.

For example, if you want to add a validation rule for the email field in the ContactFormType form model, you can define the validation rule using annotations like this:

```php
use Symfony\Component\Validator\Constraints as Assert;

class Contact
{
    /**
     * @Assert\NotBlank
     * @Assert\Email
     */
    public $email;
```

```
    }
```

In this example, the @Assert\NotBlank validation rule indicates that the email field cannot be empty, while @Assert\Email indicates that the email field must be a valid email address.

Once the validation rules are defined in the form data model, you can use the Symfony validation component to apply the validation rules to the form during form handling in the controller. For example, you can modify the contactAction controller to apply the validation rules to the email field like this:

```php
use Symfony\Component\HttpFoundation\Request;
```

```php
use Symfony\Component\Validator\Validator\ValidatorInterface;


public function contactAction(Request $request, ValidatorInterface $validator)
{
    $contact = new Contact();
    $form = $this->createForm(ContactFormType::class, $contact);

    $form->handleRequest($request);

    if ($form->isSubmitted() && $form->isValid()) {
        $errors = $validator->validate($contact);

        if (count($errors) > 0) {
```

```
        // Handle form validation errors
    } else {
        // Form data is valid, handle form submission
        }
    }


    return $this->render('contact.html.twig', [
        'form' => $form->createView(),
    ]);
}
```

In this example, the contactAction controller uses the Symfony validation component to apply the validation rules to the email field of the form. The validate() method of the validation component takes a Contact object as an argument and returns a collection of validation errors, which can be used to handle validation errors in the form.

Furthermore, Symfony offers a range of additional features for form handling, such as handling input fields, creating custom input fields, managing nested form models, and much more. These advanced features allow developers to create complex and interactive forms that meet the specific needs of their applications.

In conclusion, using forms in Symfony is essential for creating sophisticated and high-quality web applications. With the integrated form management and validation system, developers can easily and accurately create interactive and dynamic forms. With the advanced features offered by Symfony for form handling, programmers can create custom forms that meet the specific needs of their applications, while ensuring the security and reliability of user-entered data.

Symfony is a popular PHP framework that provides tools and features to help developers build powerful and secure web applications. One of the key components of Symfony is form validation, which helps ensure that user input is accurate and meets certain criteria before being processed by the application. In this article, we will explore how to use Symfony's form validation capabilities to validate user input and provide feedback to the user.

To get started with form validation in Symfony, we first need to create a form class that extends Symfony's built-in FormType class. This class will define the fields of the form and any validation rules that should be applied to those fields. Here is an example of how a simple form class might look:

```php
// src/Form/ExampleFormType.php
```

```php
namespace App\Form;

use Symfony\Component\Form\AbstractType;
use Symfony\Component\Form\FormBuilderInterface;
use Symfony\Component\OptionsResolver\OptionsResolver;
use Symfony\Component\Validator\Constraints as Assert;

class ExampleFormType extends AbstractType
{
    public function buildForm(FormBuilderInterface $builder, array $options)
    {
```

```php
        $builder
            ->add('email', EmailType::class, [
                'constraints' => [
                    new Assert\NotBlank(),
                    new Assert\Email(),
                ],
            ])
            ->add('password', PasswordType::class, [
                'constraints' => [
                    new Assert\NotBlank(),
                    new Assert\Length(['min' => 8]),
                ],
            ]);
    }

    public function configureOptions(OptionsResolver $resolver)
```

```
    {
        $resolver->setDefaults([
            'data_class' => Example::class,
        ]);
    }
}
```

In this example, we have created a form class called ExampleFormType with two fields: email and password. Each field is assigned a type (EmailType and PasswordType) and a set of validation constraints. The email field must not be blank and must be a valid email address, while the password field must not be blank and must be at least 8 characters long.

Next, we need to create a controller class that will handle the form submission and validation. Here is an example of how a controller might look:

```php
// src/Controller/ExampleController.php

namespace App\Controller;

use App\Entity\Example;
use App\Form\ExampleFormType;
use Symfony\Bundle\FrameworkBundle\Controller\AbstractController;
use Symfony\Component\HttpFoundation\Request;
use Symfony\Component\HttpFoundation\Response;

class ExampleController extends AbstractController
```

```php
{
    public function exampleAction(Request $request): Response
    {
        $example = new Example();
        $form = $this->createForm(ExampleFormType::class, $example);

        $form->handleRequest($request);

        if ($form->isSubmitted() && $form->isValid()) {
            // Process the form data
        }

        return $this->render('example.html.twig', [
            'form' => $form->createView(),
```

```
        ]);
    }
}
```

In this controller class, we first create a new instance of the Example entity and use the createForm() method to create a new form instance based on our ExampleFormType class. We then call the handleRequest() method to bind the form data to the request and validate it against the constraints defined in our form class.

If the form has been submitted and is valid, we can proceed with processing the form data. If the form is not valid, Symfony will automatically render the form again with error messages for any fields that failed validation.

Finally, we need to create a template file to

display the form to the user. Here is an example of how a template might look:

```twig
{# templates/example.html.twig #}

<form method="post">
    {{ form_start(form) }}

    {{ form_row(form.email) }}
    {{ form_errors(form.email) }}

    {{ form_row(form.password) }}
    {{ form_errors(form.password) }}

    {{ form_rest(form) }}
```

```
        <button type="submit">Submit</button>
    {{ form_end(form) }}
</form>
```

In this template file, we use the form_start() and form_end() functions to generate the opening and closing <form> tags, respectively. We then use the form_row() function to render each form field along with any error messages that may have been generated during validation.

By following these steps, you can create a powerful and secure web application using Symfony's form validation capabilities. Symfony's form validation features make it easy to ensure that user input is accurate and meets certain criteria, helping to protect your application from potential security risks.

Index

1. Introduction to Symfony pg.4

2. Symfony Installation pg.18

3. Symfony's MVC Architecture pg.24

4. Symfony Services and Containers pg.29

5. Routing in Symfony by Symfony pg.36

6. Controllers, Actions, and Twig: Symfony's Template Engine pg.43

7. The View: template and layout and The View: helper Symfony pg.53

8. The Model: Propel The data classes and The model: objects Symfony Criteria pg.61

9. Symfony's Apps directory pg.73

10. Creating Symfony Libraries pg.83

11. Creating the database in Symfony pg.97

12. Creating modules in Symfony pg.108

13. Bundle Symfony pg.124

14. Symfony Console from Symfony Dependency management with Composer Debugging Symfony applications Error and log management pg.128

15. Creation of administration in Symfony pg.138

16. Modifying Symfony's CSS and Layout pg.144

17. HTTP Requests Management Response and Rendering in Symfony pg.157

18. Using Validation Forms in Symfony pg.164

www.ingramcontent.com/pod-product-compliance
Lightning Source LLC
Chambersburg PA
CBHW050058230526
45470CB00004B/1577